Mata Hari:
Eye of the Day

Mata Hari:
Eye of the Day

Charles Rammelkamp

Apprentice House
Baltimore, Maryland

First Edition

Printed in the United States of America
Paperback ISBN: 978-1-62720-076-9
E-book ISBN: 978-1-62720-077-6

Published by Apprentice House

Apprentice House
Loyola University Maryland
4501 N. Charles Street
Baltimore, MD 21210
410.617.5265 • 410.617.2198 (fax)
www.apprenticehouse.com
info@apprenticehouse.com

This book is for Abby, the eye of my day.

In *Mata Hari: Eye of the Day*, Charles Rammelkamp has created a vivid and poignant picture of Mata Hari, the woman who has been libeled for decades as a German spy during World War I. But in Rammelkamp's skillful imagination, she's more sinned against than sinning, a woman who really wanted only to be recognized for her dancing ability, and who wanted a bit of fun thrown in, sort of a pre-Twenties Good Time Girl, in a world precarious for single women who had to live on their looks and wits. By the end, even knowing her tragic fate, we're rooting for her to somehow survive the cynical, nationalistic web that forces she can neither understand nor control have wound around her. In times of war, no one is safe, and everyone, especially the exceptional, is a potential victim and scapegoat. Rammelkamp depicts this tragic situation in vivid and evocative dramatic monologues.

> — Robert Cooperman, winner of the Colorado Book
> Award for Poetry

Charles Rammelkamp's *Eye of the Day* is a collection of smart, musical, sometimes wryly funny, sometimes heartbreaking, always entertaining poems that, when read together, tell the sweeping story of Margaretha Zelle, better known as the infamous femme fatale Mata Hari. Rammelkamp demystifies the life of the exotic dancer turned double agent, revealing the all-too-human desires and delusions behind the legend. At the same time, Eye of the Day honors Margaretha's tremendous will to survive. What I love most about these poems is that each one tells a piece of Margaretha's story in the voice of a person involved in her life or, best of all, in the voice of the woman herself, creating a prismatic view of a fascinating life touched by major events in history.

> —Alison Morse, Peacewriter, Women PeaceMakers
> Program, Joan Kroc Institute for Peace Studies
> Winner of the 2012 Tiferet Fiction Award

Charles Rammelkamp doesn't just give us a tour of a life. We have an entire time recreated for us, voices that seem familiar and not familiar all at once. *Mata Hari: Eye of the Day* is a wonderfully unified and vital collection, robust, a history that is accessible—and challenging.

—Kenneth Pobo, author of *Bend of Quiet and When the Light Turns Green*

Mata Hari: Eye of the Day is a tour de force. Not for the first time, Charles Rammelkamp's poems show the novelist's gift of inhabiting multiple characters. Each speaks his or her vignette, but the differences among them are not just of point of view and character. These prisms are moving in time as well, and each propels the drama a little further down the path as a beguiling child grows from a tortured family into sexual maturity, intrigue, tragedy and history. Each poem is complete unto itself, yet each takes its place in a galloping page turner. It radiates an aura of utterly persuasive historical and cultural detail.

— Roger Netzer, author of *Poems for Two Boys*

Acknowledgements

I would like to thank Kevin Atticks and the team at Apprentice House who helped bring this book about – Valerie Casola, Danielle Maiale, Catherine Lee. It was a pleasure working with everyone.

I would also like to thank my readers, Robert Cooperman and Alison Morse, for commenting on early drafts. Their suggestions have improved this book.

Finally, I am indebted to Patricia Shipman whose biography, *Femme Fatale*, was an invaluable resource in researching the life and intrigues of Margaretha Zelle MacLeod – Mata Hari.

Several of these poems have appeared in other publications. "Mata Hari Faces the Firing Squad" appeared in *Iodine Poetry Review*, and "Andrée Messimy Comments on Mata Hari's Trial,," "André Mornet, Prosecutor" and "Léon Bizard, Prison Doctor at Saint-Lazare" appeared in the online journal, *Misfit Magazine*.

Contents

Dysfunctional Family

The Bokkenwagon

My parents' oldest and the only girl,
I was Papa's princess, his favorite,
the center of attention.
Vain himself, owner of a successful haberdashery,
he spoiled me with flamboyant clothing,
vivid dresses of scarlet velvet.
They made my classmates jealous.
How Papa loved to be noticed!
With my dark curls and olive skin
I was his most vibrant accessory!

On my sixth birthday Papa surprised me
with an extravagant goat-drawn phaeton,
fine as the ones the wealthy drove,
the ones pulled by horses: a vehicle
to bolster his own self-importance.
Still, it distinguished me from everyone else.

"An *amazing* bit of foolishness!"
one of the citizens of Leeuwarden later declared,
"It marked Margaretha
from the start,
a girl too many noticed
for all the wrong reasons."

Adam Zelle: My Margaretha

Even when she was a child I knew
she'd break men's hearts,
love them dry -- and wet:
the hair on her head a soft brown nest,
curls boys would one day want
to bury their noses into,
dark eyes like darts
to pierce and deflate their self-assurance.

She was my darling little girl.
In the years of my triumph
I spared no expense on her education:
music, art, culture, manners, language.

Margaretha would always be elegant,
even after my decline, my disgrace.

Antje Van der Meulen: My Adam

Thirty-one when Adam proposed,
I sometimes feared
life was passing me by.

A man of ambition,
Adam surely loved me
as much as I did him,
but my social status in Franeker
must have attracted him as well.

Eventually he broke my heart,
but how glorious those ten years we had!
I remember the portrait
he had painted of himself,
on horseback, in full uniform,
as if it were etched on my brain:
that was my Adam, so full of himself,
so proud, so easily hurt.

I sometimes feared
he loved our daughter Margaretha
more than he did me.
Oh, so silly! But still,
she was his favorite of our four.

The Baron

Papa was a good-looking man.
His full beard gave him an air of royalty.
Three years before I was born,
he'd been selected to be in the Mounted Guard
when King Willem II visited Leeuwarden.

People in our town called him "the Baron,"
though it may have been from jealousy, a jibe
at his pretension, his taste for posing,
a sarcastic poke in the eye.

So when his hat factory failed,
his haberdashery went to hell,
and he had to declare bankruptcy,
the blow to his pride came twice as hard,
the schadenfreude sharp as a thorn.
He abandoned us for The Hague.

I was almost thirteen then,
on the verge of womanhood.

Abandoned

Mama died two years after Papa left us,
dragged to the grave by shame and poverty,
her heart torn apart: by then Papa lived
with another woman in Amsterdam,
Mama having to endure the snubs,
the titters, the devastating silences
of the people of Leeuwarden.

My younger brother Johannes went to live
with Mama's family in Franeker.
The twins went to Amsterdam,
to live with Papa and his new wife.

Me? I was packed off to the Vissers,
my uncle and his wife,
in the little town of Sneek.
How could Papa do this to me?
After the French lessons at Miss Buys',
the piano, the singing, the handwriting,
my exquisite manners. Why?

Susanna Catharina ten Hoove, Second Wife of Adam Zelle, on Zelle's Daughter

I fell for Adam
the moment I met him.
Such flair, such style,
and so handsome!
Yes, I heard the whispers
he was a peacock, a popinjay,
but I couldn't help myself.

Still, I put my foot down
about that daughter of his.
If Adam was vain, conceited,
Margaretha made him seem shy,
a stammering schoolboy,
and she a saucy teenager
just becoming aware
of her power over men.

The way Adam spoiled her,
she'd only have to snap her fingers
to get him to give her what she wanted,
and I could just see
those dark, gloating eyes,
taunting me.

No, I wouldn't have it.
We'd take the twins instead.
We would *not* take that daughter
into our home.
She was going to those cousins, the Vissers,
in that little Friesian town, Sneek,
No Amsterdam for that girl!
No M'Greet for me!

Headmaster Wybrandus Haanstra's New Student

At my age,
just over half a century,
I never dreamed a sixteen-year old girl
like Margaretha Zelle
would make my breath quicken,
hands sweaty as damp cloth.

Newly admitted to my boarding school in Leiden,
as a favor to my parents' friends back home in Sneek,
the Vissers, who'd been saddled with the child
when her mother in Leeuwarden died
and her father's new wife refused her in favor of the twins,
M'Greet, as she was called,
had me stammering like a schoolboy.
Relations between my wife and me
had long cooled to a comfortable affection,
but this tall, dark young woman
caused my blood to boil,
my vegetable love to grow vaster than empires.

The girl knew this, and dare I say
she took advantage of the situation?
She seemed no less attracted to me, I must admit.

Inevitable that we'd be caught,
I nevertheless couldn't resist,
so when the scandal broke,
after we'd been discovered naked
in her dormitory room,
the girl had to be sent back to the Vissers,
back to Sneek in shame,
if I were to continue my work at the school,
perfecting the Leiden kindergarten method
for which I'd become famous,
encouraging children's natural love of learning.

Mother and I reconciled as well;
my dear wife recognized M'Greet
as a bad influence.

Rudolf MacLeod's Object: Matrimony

I'd be forty my next birthday,
but sometimes I felt like I was a hundred already:
I'd spent twenty years fighting
in the Dutch East Indies, bloody wars
followed by restless peace in between,
Sumatra, Bali, Lombok, Borneo,
plagued by malaria, cholera, diabetes, typhus,
tropical parasites, even syphilis.
I was ready to settle down. Only, how?
Back home in Holland, I didn't know a soul,
unfamiliar with the finer points of the social graces:
too loud in polite company,
my language army-coarse, unrefined.

My drinking friend, de Balbian Verster,
with whom I caroused at the American Café
on the Leidseplein overlooking the canal,
in Amsterdam, sick of my complaining,
as a joke placed an ad on my behalf
in *The News of the Day:*

Officer on home leave
from Dutch East Indies
would like to meet a girl
of pleasant character –
object matrimony.

That was how I came to meet
Margaretha Zelle, my sweet Griet.

Margaretha Zelle Decides to Marry

After Papa went bankrupt –
fallen into disgrace like a disobedient angel,
having been one of Leeuwarden's
most important burghers –
he deserted us for The Hague.
I was just thirteen.

Then Mama died three years later.
My brother Johannes went to her family
in nearby Franeker, while the twins
went to stay with Papa in Amsterdam.
I'd always been his favorite,
but I was stuck with my uncle and aunt,
the Vissers, in Sneek.

They packed me off to a boarding school in Leiden
faster than a Hans Brinker.
They knew the headmaster, Wybrandus Haanstra.
Thirty-five years my senior,
married, with children,
the horny old goat made passes at me,
and what was I supposed to do,
on my own, just sixteen?
Not that I didn't encourage him.

But the scandal of our affair
was all mine. The headmaster unsullied,
I was sent home in shame.
The Vissers packed me off
to other relatives in The Hague.

I had to find a better way
to make my way in the world.
That's why I answered the ad
in *The News of the Day*,
Rudolf MacLeod, an officer on leave
from the Dutch East Indies,
twenty years older than me,
wanting to get married.

Comme Il Faut

"I know well
it is not *comme il faut,*"
I wrote Rudolf
(whom I loving addressed as "Johnie"),
after we'd already exchanged a few letters,
"but we find ourselves
in a special case, no?"

I proposed we meet.
After the affair with Headmaster Haanstra,
I'd been shuffled off to another set of relatives
in The Hague, M. and Mevr. Taconis.
The Hague was better than Sneek,
but my life was still unbearable.
I needed adventure, independence.

We arranged to meet
at the Rijksmuseum in Amstedam.
March 24, 1895, was the date.
Six days later, we were engaged.

And *that*, my dear,
is how it is done.

Retired General Norman MacLeod Passes Judgment

It seemed a little rushed to me,
but Rudolf didn't have a lot of time to dally,
and he'd proven himself a worthwhile solider,
two decades in the Indies.
He had his pick of the *nyais,* I'd have guessed,
the sweet half-caste concubines,
but apparently he wanted to take a wife back with him.

As the patriarch of the MacLeod clan,
I was called upon to approve of the girl.
I'm a shrewd judge of character,
and I sensed right away
Norman might be getting in over his head,
but what the hell,
he'd had the decency to consult me;
how could I refuse him,
even if he was a bit worse for wear,
having endured all those years in the Indies?

"Young but good-looking," I decreed, finally,
judgment wise as Solomon,
"Damn good-looking."

Gentlemen, That Lady Is My Wife

Yes, Griet was only nineteen,
less than half my age,
but still, at Wiesbaden,
where we'd gone for our honeymoon,
to see those smirking idlers
sniffing after her like a pack of dogs
nearly drove me insane,
as if I were an irrelevance,
merely a court eunuch.

The regal way she carried herself
turned men's heads as if they could spin
completely around, and Griet knew it,
the little coquette, behaving as if
we could live like people who spend
a hundred thousand guilders every year.

How she loved luxury!
To be the center of attention.
Infuriating how I had to shoo her admirers away,
me, an officer in the Dutch East Indies.

The Colorful Butterfly

I wanted to live
like a colorful butterfly, admired,
floating in the sun,
rather than bored and comfortable,
in the claustrophobic calmness
of the inside of my room,
but after our honeymoon,
penury forced us to live in Amsterdam
with Rudolf's domineering sister Louise –
or "Tante Frida," as the battleax insisted.
Rudolf's debts continued to amass,
like piles of winter snow, growing:
supporting us on his meager sick pay,
he continued to drink and carouse
as if he were still a carefree bachelor.

Oh, how critical Louise was,
because I knew nothing about housekeeping!
I was not good enough for her dear Rudolf.
She always took her brother's side,
even after he'd started whoring again.

But I? I had artistic aspirations.
I was not inclined to frugality,
was not meant to be a housewife.
I refused to live a life without luxury.

How I longed to drift away from them,
float up to the bright lights
where I belonged!

De Balbian Verster Spends an Evening with Griet

At the American Café, over a whiskey and cigar,
Rudolf suddenly pressed so close to me, smirking,
I nearly suffocated under his cloying pomade.
In a voice oozing smugness and familiarity,
he explained he had a date with two women,
that he didn't want to break,
barely able to keep the boast out of his voice,
and asked if I'd keep Griet company that evening.

So I went over to his sister's,
where they were staying.
The girl wasn't even twenty,
but she charmed me with her piano and singing,
her conversation about arts and languages,
never suspecting what Rudolf was up to.

Several hours later Rudolf returned,
posing as the perfect husband,
kissing his wife lovingly, meanwhile
winking at me over her shoulder,
sniffing his finger, his lips slick.

I wanted to kick him.

N.A. Calisch on the Repayment of a Loan

I met the newlyweds
at the Hotel and Travel Sector exposition
in Amsterdam in the summer of ninety-five.
I was chairman of the executive committee,
and I made sure they had a wonderful time,
strolling through the ornamental gardens,
the various pavilions, the life-sized model
of the ship, *Prinz Hendrick,*
MacLeod a military man and all.

He was much older than she,
a veteran of the Indies,
a decorated hero by all accounts.
I wondered if that had swayed her,
she so much younger and livelier than he.

Later, I loaned him three thousand guilders,
thinking him a man of some resources,
demonstrated initiative,
an honorable man, at any rate,
though when he later retired from the army
as a major with almost thirty years' service,
his annual pension was less than the loan.

Needless to say the scoundrel never repaid me,
though I did hear he'd asked his pretty young bride
to "be nice" to me, as a form of repayment.
I'm not sure which was the greater outrage.

Norman Is Conceived

We finally got our own place on Jacob Lennepkade,
away from the prying shrew, Tante Frida.
God, how wonderful it felt!

As if to celebrate,
a few weeks later we attended
a reception at the Royal Palace
to honor the Queen's upcoming sixteenth birthday.
Everybody remarked what a lovely couple
Rudolf and I made, me in my gown,
Rudolf with his medals and gold braid.

This was the life I envisioned!
Not staying at home, mending clothes,
preparing paltry meals for my husband.
High society was my natural milieu!
Now it seemed we two were reconciled at last;
our marriage was not a mistake after all!

Within days I was pregnant:
our first child; our son:
Norman John, in honor of the general!

Dutch East Indies

Of Rebirth, Birth, Death

Three months after Norman's birth,
we left on the *Prinses Amalia*
for the Dutch East Indies!
A new life where nobody would know
about my batty dad, my shameful affair
with horny old Headmaster Haanstra.

Rudolf spent those three months
whoring with the ladies
from "the ice skating club."
But what did I care now?
If anything his faithlessness freed me,
gave me license
to pursue my own pleasure.

The monster had already given me syphilis,
I'd discover from my own skin sores
and those on the children.
Such a man should have been deeply ashamed:
his a ruined body
that could only ruin a young woman.

We'd spend five long years in the Indies,
a liberating world
of heat, light, lush vegetation.
I now called myself Gretha,
to symbolize the change, my new identity.

My daughter Nonnie would be born there,
our loving little boy Norman would die,
poisoned, like our marriage.

My Little Miss

We lived like royalty in Java,
Rudolf promoted to major,
a vast house in Tumpang, with servants,
girdled by a verandah.

Sometimes in the evening we'd stroll,
arm in arm, through the lush parks
maintained by our gardeners,
looking back at the house
with aristocratic pride
as the servants lit the lamps,
one by one by one.

At such times I forgave Rudolf,
his bullying, his selfishness, his indiscretions,
lost in the drama of my luxurious good fortune,
and soon I was pregnant again.

This time we had a girl,
a year and a half after Norman.
Rudolf insisted we name her Jeanne Louise
after his repugnant shrew of a sister, Tante Frida,
but I only ever referred to her as Non,
short for the Javanese *nonna,*
our "little miss."
Nobody would ever call her "Louise."

Margaretha's Stage Debut

None of us under MacLeod's command
could help ogling his wife
in her low-cut purple velvet gown,
when she starred as the queen
in a production of *The Crusaders,*
to celebrate Queen Wilhelmina's coronation back home,
her highness turning eighteen, in 1898.

We all groaned with lust, sighed,
only native whores available to the likes of us,
watching her, graceful, up on the stage.

Later, we could hear MacLeod's jealous bellow,
threatening his wife, accusing her
of sleeping with every man in the audience,
overhearing our indiscreet remarks.

"You've been with all of them, haven't you?"
he thundered, anguished, impotent,
his imagination enflamed by the remarks
we all couldn't help ourselves from muttering.
A laugh, too, considering
the whoremongering MacLeod was always up to.

Mrs. van Rheede Looks out for Gretha and Her Children, 1899

Rudolf left for Medan in Sumatra, in March,
the new garrison commander there,
leaving his wife
and children with my husband and me –
my husband comptroller for the province.
A few hours before boarding the *S.S. Carpentier,*
Rudolf rode up on his horse,
and without dismounting announced
his family was coming by in a few hours
to stay with us "for about a week.
That's all right, isn't it?"

They were with us two months!
Cheap Rudolf saw a way
to put his wife in a respectable household,
spend not much money,
and prevent her from seeing other men.

When the week grew into a month,
and Gretha ran short of money,
I wrote my sister in Medan,
asking her to let Rudolf know
his wife was broke and needed clothes.

I really felt so sorry for Gretha –
intelligent, charming, if a bit frivolous –
always at a local club
surrounded by admirers.
She suffered from being married
to a much older man,
so jealous as to be her enemy.

Rudolf: Après Moi, le Déluge

We live in a bizarre world, Griet.
I work like a dog here in Deli –
you have no idea the responsibilities
of commanding the Medan garrison –
and what do you do
besides plague me for money?

One of us has all the worries,
must work hard and unhappily,
while the other doesn't do a thing
with her ten dainty fingers,
lives without concerning herself
about anyone or anything,
including the children.

Griet, when I disappear,
and you are the same useless creature,
you will cry tears of blood
for not having done your duty by me,
for not having done anything
except dressing yourself, eating and sleeping.
Listen for once to your husband, Griet:
Après moi, le Déluge!

Rudolf Welcomes His Family to Medan

What freedom I felt,
apart from that bitch.
Two glorious months!
It was like the old days,
but now she insists on queening it
over the other officers' wives
at General Reisz' going-away party,
she the wife of the new garrison commander,
Reisz' replacement, flirting like a whore
with their husbands, turning their heads.

But I'd forgive her even that
if the children didn't look so pale,
so wan and ill.
She must have neglected them in Tumpang,
whoring with soldiers behind my back.

How Griet makes me suffer!
The problem: how to disentangle myself
from such a floozy
and still keep the children?

Gretha Mourns for her Son

No more than a month in Medan
and our darling boy Norman dies!
How can this be? Not even three!

Are they true, these rumors I hear,
the babu, Norman's nursemaid,
poisoned our child
to exact revenge on Rudolf
for punishing her husband, an orderly?

How our baby suffered,
vomiting ropes of thick black liquid,
retching, in pain.
The garrison doctor suspected foul play
but Rudolf refused an autopsy,
burying our son the day he died.

And of course Rudolf blames me
for Norman's death.
This is killing me!

The Babu Confesses to her Lover

I poisoned the child
because of what MacLeod did to you,
the beating, the humiliation
you suffered for nothing,
because MacLeod is nothing
but a bully.

The child was sickly anyway,
must have suffered months of neglect,
his mother with the officers in Tumpang
while her husband was here in Medan.

How MacLeod doted on that child!
"Everything on earth to me,"
he'd declared more than once.
So the cruelest form of revenge,
to destroy something he loved.

But it wasn't just for you, my love,
I craved MacLeod's pain.
He'd forced himself on me
when his wife wasn't here,
then threw me over like so much trash.

"You'll take care of my children,"
he snarled when the family arrived,
"and you won't bother me again."

Was he punishing me
by punishing you
once he found out
you and I were lovers?

So you see, I had to punish him
far, far worse than he'd injured you or me.

Rudolf, in Denial over Norman's Death, Retires from the Military

I saved the leaves of the calendar
for June 27 and 28, the days
little Norman died and was buried,
cut a lock from his hair
as he lay in his coffin.
Oh God, why me?
How could you let this happen to me?

I don't believe the rumors
Norman's babu poisoned my boy.
Why would she do that?
Because I sent her away from my bed?
Ridiculous! How would killing Norman
possibly hurt me? No, it was my wife
who killed our baby boy,
abandoning him in Tumpang
so she could go whoring.
How ill he and Nonnie looked
the day they arrived in Medan.

So why put the little fellow through an autopsy?
It wouldn't bring him back in any case.
No, in this tropical heat he'd rot, putrefy;
instead, we held a dignified funeral,
full of military pomp and grandeur,
all the officers of the garrison attending.
My life is empty now without him.
I will never see Norman again.
So I'm leaving the military, retiring.
If I were to die myself,
my wife left to care for and educate our children,
it would have only turned out worse.
I'll try to take some solace in that.

Louise Balkstra Remembers Greta

She visited my sister Laura and me
often at Kemloko, Papa's coffee plantation,
on the slopes of the volcano,
especially after her son's tragic death.

So lively! And married
to MacLeod, that withdrawn older man.
We couldn't understand it.

Greta was not beautiful,
but so full of charm;
she danced like a goddess.
She did have splendid legs.

How she outraged Mother, though!
Always flirting with the men;
indeed, sneaking away with one of them
now and then,
returning later all disheveled,
a serene secret shining
in the depths of her dark eyes
like hidden treasure just out of reach.

"I will be celebrated,"
Greta joked to Laura and me,
though the hard look in her eyes
said she wasn't joking at all.
"Or notorious. I will die,
eventually, on the scaffold."

Gretha Writes Her Father from Sindanglaja, 1901

I am young, happy, beautiful,
still optimistic about life,
and Rudolf is old and jealous
and doesn't want anyone to look at me.

I can never love Rudolf again.
Quick-tempered as a snake,
he jumps at me with red, bloodshot eyes,
drunk and spiteful,
spits at me, threatens me
with a loaded revolver,
hits me and dares me
to strike back.

I just wish one day
I would become a widow –
ugly as it is to desire someone's death,
it just spilled from my pen
all on its own.

Escape to Amsterdam, 1902

I almost wish we'd stayed in the Indies.
First there was Rudolf's behavior
aboard the *SS Konongin Wilhelmina*,
all the way home, a brute, abusive,
and then there was Tante Frida again,
with whom we had to stay
because we were broke.

I simply cannot stand the harridan;
I came home late for dinner
every night, to avoid her,
and of course Rudolf accused me of whoring,
flaunting in public.

We finally moved out of his sister's place
to an apartment on Van Breestraat,
but then his creditors brought lawsuits.
Mr. Calisch, from whom Rudolf had borrowed
three thousand guilders six years earlier,
when we'd first married (and to whom
Rudolf, a pimp, had asked me to "be nice")
was only one of many looking
for the return of his money.

And then one day in August
Rudolf took Nonnie with him to the post office
and they vanished from Amsterdam!
He'd sneaked off to Velp
with my daughter.

Madame Goodvriend nee Baroness
Sweerts de Landas Decribes the Divorce

Two days after Rudolf kidnapped Nonnie,
Gretha filed for a divorce from my cousin
in the court of Amsterdam,
alleging that during their marriage
he beat her almost daily,
referred to her to their servants
as "that bitch of mine,"
shouted at her when he was drunk,
"I will make your life so miserable
that you will bugger off,"
thrashed her with a walking stick
until the maidservant had to intervene,
as well as other offenses,

and requesting,
should it please the court,
to grant a divorce, with the provision
he give her a monthly payment of 100 guilders
and she would come live
with my husband and me in Arnhem.

But then Rudolf put an advertisement
in the *Arnhem Daily*
that so embarrassed us,
advising any and all
not to furnish credit to his wife,
that we had to ask her to leave.
We were frankly sick of the whole mess.

Claiming poverty, my cousin Rudolf withheld the money
and Gretha had to entertain gentlemen
in *maisons de rendezvous*
to make ends meet
until Rudolf finally got his way:
Gretha agreed to let him have Nonnie,
and she would never see
her daughter again.

Superstar

Archibald Nash, Journalist: Why Paris?

When I asked Lady MacLeod, years later,
why she left Holland for Paris in 1903 –
she'd been staying with an uncle and aunt
in The Hague, modeling clothes as a mannequin –

she replied with a charming naïveté,
"I don't know.
I thought all women
who ran away from their husbands
went to Paris."

She looked for work posing for artists,
claiming to be the widow
of a Dutch East Indies soldier,
trying to support herself and two children,
but her only source of income
was pleasing men.
Ultimately, she had to return
to the Netherlands, broke.

But she'd be back.
You couldn't keep a woman
like that down.

Francis Keyzer, correspondent for a British Society Magazine, Attends a Performance by Lady Gresha MacLeod, February 4, 1905

I wangled an invitation
to the private dance at Madame Kiréevsky's,
a society hostess in Paris,
Lady Gresha MacLeod, native of Java,
performing sacred, holy dances
from the mystical East,
fusing sexuality and religion.

The private audience in its place,
she glided in, in a mass of flowers,
stood motionless, transfixed,
eyes fastened to a statue of Shiva,
all got up in an elaborate costume
of jewels and precious metals,
a casque of worked gold on her head,
an intricate breastplate beneath her arms,
a transparent white robe,
a scarf about her hips.

And then, my God,
in undulant, hypnotic, tiger-like movements
she approached the statue,
eyes shining fire, as if striving
to find favor with the god.

She became more frenzied, more feverish,
throwing off the flowers and the veils,
one by one,
until finally, in a state of frenzy,
she unclasped the belt
that held the scarf about her hips,
collapsed, naked, in a swoon at Shiva's feet!

Lady MacLeod is Venus!

Voila, Mata Hari

Following my triumph at Madame Kiréevsky's,
Emile Guimet invited me to dance
at his museum of Oriental art,
where the sacred dances of the East
wold attract an audience of the elite,
Paris' wealthiest aristocrats,
come to fawn over Oriental art
but really there for the nudity.
Well, why not? I understood this.

Monsieur Guimet made a sharp suggestion
I needed another name for the stage
instead of "Lady Gresha MacLeod."
And so Mata Hari was born,
a Malay phrase I remembered well
from my days in the Dutch East Indies.
"Sunrise," "the Eye of the Day."

Mata Hari Reviews the Reviews

Guimet transformed the museum's domed library
into an Indian temple, flowers, vines
coiling around the columns supporting the dome.
My dance was a sacred poem,
each movement a word,
every word swimming on a current of music.

The reviewers raved.
The Gallic: "Mata Hari is so feline,
extremely feminine, majestically tragic,
her body's thousand curves and movements
trembling in a thousand rhythms."

The Flash: "An exotic spectacle, yet deeply austere.
Mata Hari's flexible body takes on the shape
of the undulations of flames, then suddenly freezes
like the wavy edge of a kris."

Henri Ferrare raved in *The Press:*
Extolling my passion, my performance,
breathlessly announcing my triumph.

Ah, at last, my success!
From obscure Dutch girl,
making ends meet
in *les maisons de rendezvous*
to the talk of the town,
la belle de Paris!

The Myth

Soon I was dancing all across Europe:
the Trocadero, the Olympia Theater,
Paris, Berlin, Madrid, Monte Carlo, Vienna,
exclusive salons in private homes,
Baron de Rothschild, Gaston de Menier.

My mystique swelled, my legend grew:
the daughter of a temple dancer in India;
rescued by a Scottish lord;
"personifies all of the poetry of India,
its mysticism, its voluptuousness,
its charm ... a really paradise-like dream."

And as if there were a rivalry,
the newspapers compared me
with the celebrity dancers of the day,
Maud Allan, Isadora Duncan.
The New Vienna Journal declared:
"Isadora Duncan is dead!
Long live Mata Hari!"

The Lovers

I received the protection
of the richest strangers,
and I did not lack the skill
to profit from that,
let me assure you.

Yes, the life suited me.
I could satisfy all my caprices.
This night I dined with Count A,
the next night with Duke B,
and if I did not have to dance,
next day I took a trip with Marquis C.
I avoided serious liaisons,
legacy of MacLeod.

But I did become the mistress of several:
Jules Cambon, French ambassador in Madrid,
Lieutenant Alfred Kiepert
of the Eleventh Westphalian Hussars,
who set me up in Berlin for three years
until he returned to his wife –
leaving me comfortablr with three hundred thousand marks.
I was mistress of the married stockbroker,
Xavier Rousseau, who set me up
in a chateau near Tours,
providing me with four fine horses,
visiting me on the weekends –
and then losing my 300,000 marks!

There were others, countless others
such as my sweet Edouard Willem van der Capellan,
ten years my senior, likewise married.
He took care of my bills,
supplied me with a maidservant.

Now I was compensating
for all the abuse I suffered from MacLeod.
And I was happy.
God, was I happy!

Leon Bakst, Costume Designer: Over the Hill?

What was she, thirty six, thirty-seven?
A dancer six or seven years already?
Okay, she looked great for a woman
who'd given birth to two kids,
but when Mata Hari came to Monte Carlo
to talk to Diaghilev
about performing with the Ballet Russe,
I had to nix the idea
after I examined her nude:
her figure a bit too matronly.

Still, I didn't want to offend.
I remembered when she danced
the role of Cleopatra in *Antar.*
When the opera moved to the Odeon in Paris,
Andre Antoine, the director, fired her
for putting on too much weight.
She sued for breach of contract and won.

A proud woman, I'd hate to cross her.

The Real Madame Rousseau

My husband was very good-looking
but also a skirt-chaser.
So I shouldn't have been surprised
when he took Mata Hari as his mistress.

First he installed her in a hotel in Paris,
then he rented a chateau in the country for her
where she lived until 1912
as "Madame Rousseau."

Neither my mother-in-law nor I
could persuade Xavier to give her up.
His mother even went out to the chateau
to state her case to Mata Hari,
only to be charmed by the woman,
leaving her there six months later,
still in charge of her chateau.

Later, Mata Hari and Xavier moved
to a mansion at Neuilly-sur-Seine,
bringing their horses and carriage with them.
Mata Hari was often seen in the mornings
riding her magnificent horses in the Bois de Boulogne.

But alas, Xavier didn't have a head for business;
he made bad investments, went bankrupt,
losing all of Mata Hari's wealth as well,
the fortune a previous lover, Herr Kiepert, had given her.

So she dumped him,
and when at long last
Xavier came back to me,
the real Madame Rousseau,
he was ruined.
I took Xavier back, of course.
What other choice did I have?

Money

It was always a problem.
I took in a great deal --
three thousand francs a month
for my role as Venus
in Marenco's *Bacco e Gambrinus* at La Scala
and likewise in Milan for dancing
"The Princess and the Flower"
in Gluck's opera, *Armide* --

but I spent a great deal, too.
I had a lifestyle to maintain, after all,
and after Xavier Rousseau squandered
my private fortune,
I'd had to return to the theater.

When I asked my agent, Gabriel Astruc,
if he knew anyone
"who would be interested in the protection
of an artist," as a sort of investment –
I needed thirty thousand francs right away
to pay some bills and to provide
the necessary tranquility so vital to my art –
I'm afraid it may have sounded
as if I were asking him to be my pimp –
I *had* been going with certain men
to *maisons de rendezvous* to get a little cash.

But really, what is an agent for
if not to make a girl some money?

Deutschland Uber Alles!

Strapped for money, I danced for low pay
in musical comedies in Paris. I needed
a new act to capture the zeitgeist.

So I retuned to Berlin in 1914
to research a new dance,
based on ancient Egyptian culture,
at the top-flight German museums,
and although at the time
the mistress of Constant Bazet,
a Parisian banker, I resumed relations
with Alfred Kiepert, my old lover
who had set me up so well.

I signed a contract to dance
for six months, at the Metropol,
48,000 marks, starting in September.
But then things turned ugly.

"Deustschland uber alles!" the mob chanted
outside the Emperor's palace.
All foreigners were animals.

Not heeding the warnings of my lovers,
including the chief of police, Herr Griebel,
I was stuck in Germany when war broke out.
The Germans confiscated my money and furs
because I was a long-time resident of France,
with whom Germany was at war.

Fortunately I was able to charm a Dutch businessman
into paying my fare back to Amsterdam.
Later I assured his wife
I did not try to seduce him.
"I had only one chemise left," I explained.
The Germans had taken all my clothing.
"And really, I didn't feel clean
enough to make love."

Ever in 1915

I.

Back in Holland with Edouard,
I was bored.
He set me up in The Hague.
I redecorated the house at 16 Nieuwe Uitleg,
But how I longed for Paris!
For the excitement, the luxury!
Van de Capellan was a dear,
but he only visited me on the weekends.
No glamor anywhere in times of war,

II.

In March, ten years after my debut
at the Musee Guimet,
I appeared on the cover of *De Graciuse,*
the Dutch fashion magazine,
no longer in the bloom of my youth,
but my decolletage was scandalous!
The final photograph in my scrapbook.

III.

The German consul came calling,
Karl Kroemer, from Amsterdam,
an offer to become a German spy!
Giving me three bottles of invisible ink
and twenty thousand francs,
he instructed me in espionage,
even gave me a code name!
Oh, so cloak and dagger,
so *de cape et d'épée*

But when Kroemer left,
I tossed out the invisible ink,
kept the francs: repayment from Germany
for confiscating my furs and assets.

IV.

In December I danced in The Hague
at the Royal Theater, to music
by Francois Cooperin,
but I didn't drop my veils.
I was forty years old now,
and those days were gone.

When the show moved to Arnhem,
where Rudolf and Non lived,
I so hoped I'd see my daughter,
but I never did again. Ever.
It was my last performance. Ever.

Return to Paris

I could bear The Hague no longer.
Paris lured me like a butterfly to light.
I told Edouard I was only going
to collect my belongings from Neuilly,
to ship them to The Hague,
but I kept finding excuses to stay.
I renewed an old love affair
with Henri de Marugerie,
good enough reason as any to linger.

Staying at the Grand Hotel,
I began a relationship with a Belgian officer,
the Marquis de Beaufort.
The dear man was heartbroken
when at last I had to leave.

For I finally couldn't put off
my return to The Hague any longer,
bringing with me
ten crates of silver, linen and furniture.

But I went by way of Spain and Portugal,
and another lover, Emilio Junoy,
the Spanish senator.

But The Hague was as dull in 1916
as it had been the year before
when that horrible little man
detained me at Folkestone.
I just had to get away again.
Paris called to me like a lover,
full of danger and promise.

Endgame

Frank Bickers, British Police Sergeant, Questions Mata Hari at the Port of Folkestone, December 1915

Marguerite Gertrude Zelle, 39,
arrived at Folkestone
by the Dieppe boat-train,
where we questioned her.
She said she was en route to Paris
to sell her effects from the house at Neuilly.

We searched Zelle thoroughly,
found nothing incriminating,
but she is regarded by Police and Military
to be (shall we say)
not above suspicion.
Her subsequent movements *should be watched,*
and she should be refused permission
to return to the United Kingdom.

Frank Bickers Knocks Back a Pint After Work

She's a whore.
Not exactly the picture of moral rectitude, innit?

Oh, I remember the stories,
stripping off in hoity-toity cabarets
while dancing some fancy
so-called religious rites
for high-powered politicians,
playboys, aristocrats, royalty, rich people,
just there to see a pair of bristols and a beard.

But she's still a whore,
and a whore will do anything
for money, for whatever
she thinks will get her ahead.

No, it's no stretch of the imagination
to see her spying for the Germans
or for whoever'll pay her.
That's exactly how whores behave,
and Mata Hari -- or "Lady
Gresha MacLeod" (oh, blimey!) --
is nothing but a whore.

Georges Ladoux, Head of French Intelligence, Sets His Sights on Mata Hari

When I received the warning
from the British
Mata Hari was under suspicion,
perhaps a German spy,
I decided I had to bring her down,
and the best way to do that
was to recruit her to spy for France.
That way we'd watch her every move,
root her out like a pig snuffling truffles,
red-handed, with the goods.

If she'd spy for us,
she'd spy for Germany, too.
She's a foreigner, no sense of loyalty
to anybody but herself.
In other words, a whore.

And like a whore, she demanded
a million francs! For that kind of money
she'd have to penetrate German headquarters,
obtain information from a knowledgeable source.

"I have already been the mistress
of the Crown Prince," she boasted,
nostrils quivering, imperious,
"and I can do with him what I will.
The Germans adore me.
They treated me like a queen,
whereas among you French,
I am nothing but a tart."

Georges Ladoux on a Whore in Love

Mata Hari claimed to have fallen
for the Russian officer, Vladimir de Massloff,
a boy eighteen years her junior,
and he for her.

Well, why not? She'd married a brute
twice her age, lost one child,
denied access to the other,
lived as a kept woman for ten years.
Maybe she was lonely.

She'd met Vadime at Madame Dangeville's salon
in Paris, the end of July --
a retired actress who entertained officers.
They'd gone for a promenade in the Bois de Boulogne,
dined at the Pavillon d'Armenville,
then she'd taken him home to the Grand Hotel.
Nothing new in this: she'd done it
with hundreds of others before.

But when she met Vadime in Vittel
a month later,
a bandage over his left eye
where he'd been injured by mustard gas
fighting at the front, she cried,
"I will never leave you!"
Ever the actress.

So I nearly spit
when, in demanding a million francs,
Mata Hari declared,
"I have no interest except marrying my lover!"

My Darling Vadime

I've never been crazy
for a man before. And so young!
Could that really be the attraction?
Or his aristocratic Russian bearing?
Whatever it is, I feel an overpowering need
to be with him, to touch, to love him.

We met the end of July
at Madame Dangeville's salon,
and though he returned to the front
the fourth of August,
we knew we loved each other,
the Platonic puzzle pieces fitting together,
locking us in place.

I pined for Vadime during all of August,
bought him a silver cigarette case
at Walewyk, the jewelry store,
had my portrait taken for him
by countless photographers,
wrote to him incessantly.

I was desperate to be with Vadime,
but I continued to entertain officers.
I still needed money, after all,
and money meant lovers.

Tarlet and Monier on Mata Hari's Tail, Summer 1916

Ordered to follow Mata Hari around Paris
by Captain Ladoux of the Deuxieme Bureau –
the service discredited for botching the Dreyfuss Affair –
we trailed her everywhere,
like a brace of bloodhounds sniffing the ground,
trying to prove she was a German spy.
We steamed open her mail;
questioned porters, waitresses, hairdressers;
collected abundant evidence of her love affairs,
but sadly, nothing of espionage.

She was *très elegant.*
We followed her to restaurants, dressmakers,
furriers, jewelers all over Paris.

"Who are those two men?" she complained
to the bellboy at the Grand Hotel,
pointing us out as we lounged in the lobby.
A pair of Paris inspectors.

We continued to follow her,
recording her many affairs.
No sooner did the Marquis de Beaufort
leave the Grand Hotel
after a week with her in July
than she was with Bernard Antoine,
purveyor of fine liquors,
as well as with a lieutenant
of the Eighth Chasseurs d'Afrique.
Jean Hallaume, another military man—
oh, she had a soft spot for military men! –
Hallaume likewise infatuated with our *femme fatale.*
He spent a couple of hours with her daily in August,
time enough for a quick tryst.

And then there was the Russian boy,
Vladimir de Massloff – "Vadime" –
half her age, the one she claimed
she truly fell for, wanted to settle down with.
But you can't trust a whore
in affairs of the heart, can you?

Sometimes she gave us the slip,
hailing taxis and carriages
that made abrupt turns,
winking as she passed us
going in the opposite direction.

But we never got the goods on her.
At her trial, we could only testify
to her extravagant ways, her influential men.
Not a shred of evidence about espionage.

Mata Hari Goes to Vittel

How desperate I was to be with Vadime,
to touch him, bask in his youth.
We'd pledged ourselves to each other:
mad impulse; it could never be.

If ever there were star-crossed lovers!
His father, the Admiral, Russian aristocrat,
would forbid the match at the start.

But I so longed to re-unite with my lover
at Vittel, the health spa in Lorraine,
so near the front at Verdun,
travel there required official permission.

Desperation drove me to agree,
in principle, to spy for Ladoux
if he authorized my visit to Vittel
for the "cure" there.

And then, when at last, in September
Vadime and I were together again,
how his injury devastated me!
What if he were to become blind?

"Would you marry me?" he implored.

"I will never leave you!" I declared.

Crazy Mission, 1916

Following Ladoux's plan,
I sailed for Spain in November,
but when the ship docked in Falmouth,
the British were all over me
like mosquitoes sucking blood,
searching, interrogating, finally sending me
to London for further questions.

For four days they interrogated me,
trying to trip me up with stupid questions,
force a confession.
Finally, after four days, they released me,
but when I applied for a permit
to go to The Hague, "to marry
Captain Vadime de Massloff,"
I was not allowed back into Holland.
They insisted I go to Spain as planned.

In December I finally arrived in Spain,
but since I was in Madrid,
I could not get to the Crown Prince,
nor to General von Bissing, the military general
in charge of occupied Belgium,
as I'd promised Ladoux.
I had to improvise.

So I contacted a Captain von Kalle,
seduced him and got information
about German submarines off the coast of Morocco,
passed this on to the French,
returned, at last, to Paris, in January,
the beginning of 1917,
triumphant in my mission,
expecting to be paid.

In Paris, I checked into the Hotel Plaza Athenée
and immediately went to have my hair tinted.
More gray all the time.

Police Commissioner Albert Priolet Arrests Mata Hari, February 13, 1917

With a warrant for her arrest
and a detailed search of her belongings --
signed by the Minister of War himself --
I knocked at the door of Mata Hari's room
at the Élysées Palace Hotel,
accompanied by five inspectors.

We found her at breakfast
lounging in her dressing gown
(despite the vicious rumors
that she greeted us completely naked).

I read her the warrant for her arrest,
and while Mata Hari dressed,
my men turned her apartment upside down,
itemizing suspicious objects and documents,
such as visas and residence and travel permits,
photographs, addresses, correspondence,
placing them under seal.

Then we escorted Mata Hari
to the Palace of Justice, where,
at eleven o'clock,
she entered the office of the Grand Inquisitor,
our nickname for Pierre Bouchardon,
the Investigative Magistrate.

Pierre Bouchardon, Investigative Magistrate: She Was a Born Spy

From the very first interview
I had the intuition
I was in the presence of a person
who was in the pay of our enemy.

Feline, supple, artificial,
used to gambling everything and anything
without scruple, without pity,
always ready to devour fortunes,
leaving her ruined lovers
to blow their brains out.
In other words, a whore, like my wife,
who'd left *me* to blow *my* brains out --
Mata Hari was a born spy.

As Robespierre wisely noted,
"Justice must know neither friend nor parents.
She grinds in front of her
all those who are guilty."
I would grind her to dust!

I sent the whore to Saint-Lazare
to give her a taste of what awaited her,
to break her spirit,
to hammer her into submission,
grind her in the mill of justice indeed.

When I told her she was going to prison,
a haggard look came over her eyes,
dumb with fear.
Thick lips, dark skin, she resembled a savage.
Bits of dyed hair stuck out at her temples.
With satisfaction, I saw that I had broken her.

Bouchardon and The Triple Liaison

Mata Hari made me want to vomit
when she professed her great love
for the Russian dupe, de Massloff,
that gullible young idiot.

Already the official mistress
of the Dutch Colonel van der Capellan,
mistress of the Belgian commandant,
the Marquis de Beaufort,
she now presented herself as the fiancée
of Captain Vladimir de Massloff,
for whom she played the comedy of great love,
right out of an opera.

Yet even this triple liaison didn't stop the whore
from having affairs with a Montenegrin officer,
an Italian, two Irish, three or four English,
and five French officers.
Dear God! Had she no shame?

On the contrary, she boasted!
"I love officers," she declared,
her voice a simpering tart's.
"I would rather be the mistress of a poor officer
than a rich banker. My greatest pleasure
is to go to bed with them without thinking of money,
to compare the different nationalities."

What an absolute whore!
At least my wife deceived me with only one --
only one that I found out about.

Boumchardon: Fifty-Three Men!

We discovered cards and letters
in Mata Hari's rooms from fifty-three men!
Fifty-three! The mind boggles.

We questioned them all.
Of course they all claimed
she was a lovely, charming woman.
What else would you expect from them?
Especially from the married ones,
embarrassed their names might appear
in the newspapers and court proceedings.

None of them would admit
any action on Zelle's part
even hinting at espionage.
Of course they were covering for themselves.
"We only spoke of art."
Do they think I was born yesterday?

She had sexual relations with officers,
"without regard to their rank,
from all armies," Ladoux,
the Deuxieme Bureau chief testified.

With a moral character like that,
how could she *not* be a spy?

721 44625

Bouchardon sent me to the vilest prison in Paris,
Saint Lazare, originally a prison
for streetwalkers with venereal disease.
Rat-infested, filthy, dank, no heat,
lice in the pillows.
They assigned me a number, 721 44625.

I was M'Greet in Leeuwarden,
in the old brick house on Groot Kerkstraat,
Daddy's precious darling.
MacLeod called me Griet, or Greta,
and after Norman John was born
and we sailed for the Dutch East Indies,
I called myself Gretha,
to signal my transformation,
a mark of some independence from Rudolf.

Back in Europe, five years later,
I became Lady Gresha MacLeod,
an exotic dancer, woman of mystery,
and then I was Mata Hari
for ten glorious years.

To my darling Vadime I am Marina,
the most blissful of my identities.

The German, Kroemer, assigned me
the code name H21,
and now I am just another number,
and Mata Hari is dead.

Bouchardon Assesses Mata Hari's Attorney, Edouard Clunet

Clunet was an old fool,
sniffing after Mata Hari
like an out-to-pasture bull,
just a star-struck old man
at the feet of the exotic dancer.

He's been representing her interests
over ten years now,
since her first success in 1905.
He obviously turns a blind eye
to her crimes and indiscretions.

He carries out her defense
with the sickening ardor
of a neophyte, an amateur way out of his league,
displaying an inexplicable tenderness
toward the frivolous hussy,
practically drooling over the whore.

"She's in a pathological state
of anxiety," he wrote me,
shrill as a schoolgirl
whose pigtails have been pulled.
"She coughs up blood.
Her life is in danger.
Saint-Lazare is filthy, inhumane.
Could you please grant a hospital room
to this sick lady
who poses no risk of flight?"

Oh, my heart bleeds!
Clunet even knew she was in Berlin itself
when the war broke out,
the mistress of two officers *and*
the chief of police! My God!
He *knows* she's a whore!

Vadime Writes to Mata Hari from a Hospital in Epernay the Day of her Arrest

Dearest Marina,

I have been in hospital five days
for an operation on my throat.
I need so much to have you
close to me, to whisper words of love.

Alas, the distance that separates us
obliges me to do nothing
except to think of you.
I visit you in dreams
so strong I forget it's only a dream.
I open my arms to embrace you,
only to have the vision disappear.
Your photograph never leaves me,
even when I go into battle.

Please come to me in Epernay.
My kisses and thoughts are with you.
I cover your splendid body with kisses.

Your Lover Always,
Vadime

I Am Going Mad!

For three months now
I have been locked up in this dingy cell.
I am going mad!
I cry from fear in the night,
and nobody can hear me.
I am nearly dying from the filth,
the lack of care for my body,
the disgusting food they set out for me,
in a bowl, as if I were a dog.

Stop this, Monsieur Bouchardon, I beg you!
I've always been an honest woman,
well-received wherever I go.
Yes, I accepted money, in Holland,
but I did nothing for the Germans!
I considered it repayment
for the furs they seized from me.
I am innocent!

Vadime's Goodbye

Granted three days' leave in March,
I flew to Paris to find my Marina.
I hadn't heard from her in weeks.
Did she no longer love me?
I couldn't believe this, not after Vittel,
not after our declarations of love.

Baffled and alarmed by her silence,
as in a dream I tore through the Grand Hotel,
last place I knew she'd stayed,
questioning the staff, searching the rooms,
buried under the weight of my futility.
But she was gone.

Was it my surgery, the diphtheria
I'd contracted at the front?

Only later, when Bouchardin questioned me
in the hospital in Rennes,
and I'd learned about her arrest,
did I invent the story
I'd gone to Paris to break up with her.

Still, when Bouchardin tried to pin spying on her,
I didn't betray my love.
"In the course of my relationship with her,"
I said in my deposition,
"I never saw anything that was suspect.
We had a lengthy correspondence,
but she never asked for military information."

André Bellanger Accompanies Mata Hari to the Palace of Justice

We finally moved Mata Hari
out of Saint-Lazare, after five months,
but only for a few days,
and only to the Conciergerie,
to be closer to the Palace of Justice.

 I accompanied her four days later
across the courtyards,
up the magnificent spiral staircase
to the second floor courtroom
where her trial was to take place.

She looked haggard, defeated,
No longer the glamorous dancer,
her hair a dirty rat's nest,
no make-up, her face drawn.
She'd lost too much weight.

But she still carried herself like a dancer,
supple, fluid, undulant,
her back straight, her head high,
and I still knew so well
what about her had electrified my blood
over these last ten years.

Andrée Messimy Comments on Mata Hari's Trial

I'm sure the hussy had nothing
to do with the Germans.
Ridiculous to think such a woman
could traffic in international political intrigue.
She only cared for luxury and license.

But when my husband Alfred received
the summons to testify on her behalf,
I'd have died before I let him describe
the idyllic nights he'd spent in her company.

Yes, as Minister of War when the war began,
his testimony might have carried weight,
but I refused to allow our name
and his career to suffer for such a woman.

I sent a letter to Alfred-Ernest Semprou,
president of the tribunal, claiming
my husband too ill with rheumatism
to appear in court, and besides, I avowed,
he had *never* met Mata Hari in his life,
and as a finishing touch, I signed my name
with a flourish: Andrée Messimy, née Bonaparte.

After this categorical denial
of an affair with Mata Hari,
suspicion turned to Louis Malvy,
Minister of the Interior,
as the lover in question.
His political career was ruined as a result.

I didn't even have to say to my Alfred,
"I told you so." He was grateful to me,
even though I heard his heartfelt sighing.

Sex and Espionage

I've always thrived on the admiration of men.
But a spy? Me?
Yet three time since the war began
I've been asked to spy for some country;
first Karl Kroemer,
honorary German consul in Amsterdam,
recruiting agents on behalf of Germany,
paid me twenty thousand francs
and assigned me a code name, H21.
How could I refuse the money?
The Germans had already seized
my furs and valuables when war broke out.
This was simple repayment;
I never gave him information.

Then Ladoux, a fat little man
with a black beard and spectacles,
a cigarette pasted to his lips,
recruited me to spy for France.
I agreed to go to Madrid
where I gathered information
from a German army attaché, Captain Kalle,
encouraging him with certain favors,
rewarding him with certain charms.
But Ladoux would doublecross me,
making me out to be a double agent.

Martial Cazeaux also invited me
to spy for Russia when we met
at the Hotel Continental in Vigo.
A Frenchman, Cazeaux was Dutch consul.
I neither accepted nor declined.

Why did they want me as a spy?
I had no political convictions.
A conspicuous celebrity, a striking beauty:
shouldn't they have sought someone non-descript?
Was it my willingness to sleep with men for money?
Did this make me a likely spy?

Edouard Clunet Describes the Trial

The trial lasted two days
but we might just as well
have skipped it altogether.
The French were losing to the Germans.
They needed someone to blame.
Mata Hari was the perfect scapegoat
in her low-cut blouse, her saucy walk.
She'd not only killed fifty thousand Frenchmen,
her shrill busybody enemies claimed,
she'd stolen them from their wives,
led a life of breathtaking extravagance
while ordinary people went without bread.

Mornet accused Mata Hari of killing
fifty thousand Frenchmen, a figure
pulled out of thin air, no evidence
to show what she did or how that resulted.

"My defense is to speak the truth,"
she declared in closing remarks,
"I am not French.
I have the right
to have friends in other countries,
even those at war with France.
I remain neutral.
I count on the good hearts of French officers."

Alas, it wasn't enough.

André Mornet, Prosecutor

Between you and me, there wasn't enough evidence
to flog a cat.
Still, she was just a whore, nobody to get upset about,
and she *had* taken scores of German lovers in Berlin
before the war broke out.

Still, Bouchardon, the investigative magistrate
hadn't been able to prove a connection
between Mata Hari's actions and the torpedoing
of the ship in the Mediterranean,
the death of fifty thousand children,
as had been charged.

I called five witnesses.
The bumbling Paris inspector, Monier,
could only testify to her extravagant lifestyle,
But Ladoux and his boss, Goubet, the French spymasters,
explained their plan to unmask Mata Hari
as a German agent
by enrolling her as a spy for France.
Of course, Ladoux was arrested
as a German spy himself
four days after Mata Hari's execution.

Vladimir de Masloff, her Russian lover boy,
and Lieutenant Hallaure, her other summer lover,
could not attend the tribunal,
but we read their depositions aloud.
Massloff maintained she'd never asked him
for any military information.

Clunet, her defense attorney, called various influential men
to testify as character witnesses –
they'd all fucked her, of course.
"We spoke only of art," they testified.

In summing up, I declared,
"The evil that this woman has done
is unbelievable. This is perhaps
the greatest woman spy of the century."

The tribunal deliberated only forty-five minutes
before returning with a verdict of guilt.

Edouard Clunet Describes the Sentence

With the gaudy pomp and fanfare
of a court scene in a cheap opera,
the tribunal pronounced guilt
on all charges. The punishment?

"Today, the twenty-fifth of July, 1917,
the Third Permanent Council of War in Paris
has declared Zelle, Marguerite, Gertrude,
called Mata Hari,
divorcée of Mr. MacLeod,
guilty of espionage and
intelligence with the enemy.
In consequence, the aforementioned Council
condemns her to pain of death."

The Paris newspapers went wild, a blood frenzy.
"It's impossible! It's impossible!" they reported
Mata Hari's hoarse whisper to me,
sitting beside her in the courtroom,
describing her "a sinister Salomé who played
with the heads of our soldiers
in front of the German Herod."
They cast her in the role
of a biblical seductress, heartless killer:
the farce complete: a whore.

The public howled for her blood,
strident, high-pitched as the audience in the pit,
in a frenzy of self-righteous fury.
Her fate? The firing squad.

A.J. Kooij Writes to Mata Hari "a Vincennes"

She'd been condemned to death
six weeks earlier
when the idea hit me like a locomotive.
I hoped there would still be time.

If I could secure the rights
to publish her memoirs,
I'd make myself a tidy little fortune.
People would be climbing over each other
to get a copy,
and not just here, in Holland,
 but all over Europe!

Of course, living in Sneek,
I knew the Vissers, how mortified
they were by their niece's notoriety --
we all knew the story of the headmaster,
when she was blossoming teenager -
but they'd flock to the bookstore
along with the rest of them.

I knew she must be working on them --
what else did she have to do
besides make her hopeless appeals?
So in September I wrote her,
hoping to play on her hometown sympathies,
but I never got a reply.

Then again, I hadn't really
known where to write her,
had addressed the letter "a Vincennes" –
the execution ground.

President Poincare Rejects Mata Hari's Appeal for Pardon

She spent her forty-first birthday, August 7,
in the dreary filth of Saint-Lazare
while our appeals were all shot down,
one after the other,
like so many children's boats in a tub,
starting with the Dutch ambassador's request
that her punishment be reduced to a prison sentence.
In September, the Supreme Court of Appeals
upheld the denial.

She wrote the Dutch legatee in Paris
begging him to intervene,
request a presidential pardon.

As her attorney,
I consulted with the Dutch envoy;
a request for clemency came from The Hague
"for reasons of humanity."

I received Poincarte's rejection October 13.
The order for her execution was signed the next day.
Frantic, I even suggested Mata Hari
claim to be pregnant –
by me, old Edouard Clunet.

Ah, if only…if only….

Léon Bizard, Prison Doctor at Saint-Lazare

I'd come across Mata Hari once
in a house in the quarter of *L'Etoile*
when I was checking prostitutes for syphilis.
She'd been rather pricy then, I recall,
fifty louis for what they called a "passing fancy,"
rather regal and refined in such an environment.

She'd retained her grace in Saint-Lazare,
the prison in Paris reserved
for the vilest female criminals.
With an air of elegance,
despite the appalling conditions –
dark, filthy, over-run by rats,
a flea-infested straw mat to sleep on –
she greeted me like a queen
whenever I came to check on her

I knew she'd been having trouble sleeping,
and when I learned she was going to die
the following morning,
I visited her with Sister Leonide,
asked her about dancing,
and when we insisted,
she arose and performed for a few minutes.

While she was preoccupied,
I slipped a sleeping potion
into her water. At least
she would have one good sleep
before she faced the firing squad.

Mata Hari Faces the Firing Squad

Twelve men from the Fourth Regiment of Zouaves
in their khaki uniforms and red fezes,
the sergeant major of the Twenty-third Dragoons
in his navy blue uniform, black beret.
How young they look, how nervous.
They will have to live with the burden
of executing me, for the rest of their lives.

I refuse to be tied to the stake.
I decline the blindfold.
I wave to the weeping nuns.
I blow a kiss to the priest –
impossible to resist a last naughty gesture.

Captain Thibaut reads the sentence:
"By the Order of the Third Council of War
the woman Zelle has been condemned
to death for espionage."

"By God," the sergeant-major marvels,
"This lady knows how to die."

Apprentice
House Press
Loyola University Maryland

Apprentice House is the country's only campus-based, student-staffed book publishing company. Directed by professors and industry professionals, it is a nonprofit activity of the Communication Department at Loyola University Maryland.

Using state-of-the-art technology and an experiential learning model of education, Apprentice House publishes books in untraditional ways. This dual responsibility as publishers and educators creates an unprecedented collaborative environment among faculty and students, while teaching tomorrow's editors, designers, and marketers.

Outside of class, progress on book projects is carried forth by the AH Book Publishing Club, a co-curricular campus organization supported by Loyola University Maryland's Office of Student Activities.

Eclectic and provocative, Apprentice House titles intend to entertain as well as spark dialogue on a variety of topics. Financial contributions to sustain the press's work are welcomed. Contributions are tax deductible to the fullest extent allowed by the IRS.

To learn more about Apprentice House books or to obtain submission guidelines, please visit www.apprenticehouse.com.

Apprentice House
Communication Department
Loyola University Maryland
4501 N. Charles Street
Baltimore, MD 21210
Ph: 410-617-5265 • Fax: 410-617-2198
info@apprenticehouse.com • www.apprenticehouse.com